BEST OF
Bavaria
✶ ✶ ✶ ✶ ✶
Bayern

INHALT
CONTENTS

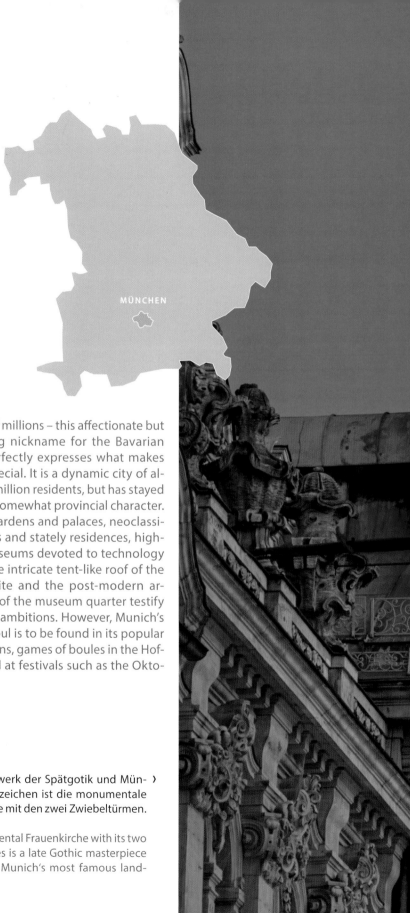

München
Munich

Millionendorf – der zugleich liebevoll wie herablassend gemeinte Spitzname für die bayerische Landeshauptstadt trifft München Besonderheit auf den Punkt: Die Metropole mit den knapp zwei Millionen Einwohnern ist dynamisch, dabei aber ihrem etwas provinziellen Charakter treu geblieben. Barocke Gärten und Schlösser, klassizistische Plätze und Paläste, hochkarätige Museen für Technik und Kunst, das filigrane Zeltdach des Olympiageländes und die postmoderne Architektur des Museumsviertels stehen für die Ambitionen einer Großstadt. Ihr gemächliches Herz aber schlägt in den beliebten Biergärten, bei den Boulespielern im Hofgarten und auf Volksfesten wie dem Oktoberfest.

A village of millions – this affectionate but patronising nickname for the Bavarian capital perfectly expresses what makes Munich special. It is a dynamic city of almost two million residents, but has stayed true to its somewhat provincial character. Baroque gardens and palaces, neoclassical squares and stately residences, high-calibre museums devoted to technology and art, the intricate tent-like roof of the Olympic site and the post-modern architecture of the museum quarter testify to big-city ambitions. However, Munich's leisurely soul is to be found in its popular beer gardens, games of boules in the Hofgarten and at festivals such as the Oktoberfest.

Ein Meisterwerk der Spätgotik und Münchens Wahrzeichen ist die monumentale Frauenkirche mit den zwei Zwiebeltürmen. ›

The monumental Frauenkirche with its two onion domes is a late Gothic masterpiece and one of Munich's most famous landmarks.

‹ Mit dem größten Volksfest der Welt, dem Oktoberfest, beginnt in München in der zweiten Septemberhälfte der Ausnahmezustand.

The world's largest festival, the Oktoberfest, transforms Munich in the second half of September.

‹ Die Feldherrnhalle am Odeonsplatz ist der Florentiner Loggia dei Lanzi nachempfunden. Mit dem üppig-goldgelben Barock der Theatinerkirche strahlt sie mediterranes Flair aus.

The Feldherrnhalle on Odeonsplatz is modelled on the Loggia dei Lanzi in Florence. Together with the sumptuous golden-yellow Baroque appearance of the Theatinerkirche, it radiates a Mediterranean atmosphere.

‹ Ältester und prunkvollster Raum der Residenz ist das 66 Meter lange, mit Renaissancefresken geschmückte Antiquarium.

The oldest and most magnificent room in the Residenz is the 66-metre-long Antiquarium with its Renaissance frescoes.

« Brunnen mit Skulpturen bekannter Münchner Volksschauspieler, hier Karl Valentin, schmücken den Viktualienmarkt.

Fountains with sculptures of well-known Munich actors adorn Viktualienmarkt – here Karl Valentin.

« Der Marienplatz mit dem Neuen Rathaus ist Münchens gute Stube. Im Vergleich zu dem mächtigen neugotischen Bau wirkt die 400 Jahre ältere Frauenkirche immer noch sehr imposant.

Marienplatz, site of the Neues Rathaus, is Munich's most popular public square. Compared to this massive neo-Gothic city hall, the 400 years older Frauenkirche is still highly impressive.

« »In München steht ein Hofbräuhaus ...« – die Hymne auf das seit 1607 bestehende Traditionswirtshaus erklingt im großen Festsaal mehrmals am Tag.

»In Munich stands a Hofbräuhaus ...« – this anthem to the traditional tavern, which dates back to 1607, rings out several times a day in the great hall there.

‹ Die mannshohen Figuren des Glockenspiels am Rathausturm führen zweimal am Tag ein Ritterturnier und den Schäfflertanz auf.

The life-size figures of the glockenspiel on the city hall tower perform a knights tournament and the barrel-makers' dance twice daily.

≫ Anfang des 19. Jahrhunderts ließ König Ludwig I. das Siegestor errichten.

King Ludwig I commissioned construction of this triumphal gate in the early 19th century.

‹ Das 2009 eröffnete Museum Brandhorst ist das architektonische Highlight des Museumsareals.

The Museum Brandhorst, opened in 2009, is the architectural highlight of the quarter known as the Museumsareal.

⌃ Schloss Nymphenburg diente ab dem 17. Jahrhundert als Sommerresidenz der bayerischen Herrscher. Hier wurde Ludwig II. geboren.

Nymphenburg Palace was the summer residence of the rulers of Bavaria from the 17th century. Ludwig II was born here.

» Rund um den klassizistischen Monopteros im Englischen Garten sind die Sonnenplätze besonders begehrt. Die im 18. Jahrhundert angelegte Parkanlage ist mit vier Quadratkilometern Fläche Münchens schönstes Grün.

Sunny spots around the classical Monopteros in the English Garden are highly prized. This park, laid out in the 18th century, is Munich's most beautiful, with an area of four square kilometres.

» Im Biergarten am Chinesischen Turm treffen Bayern auf Touristen, Studenten auf Handwerker, Manager auf Globetrotter und genießen in trauter Eintracht auf über 7000 Sitzplätzen das Bier der Hofbräu-Brauerei.

With more than 7000 seats, the beer garden by the Chinese Tower is where Bavarians meet tourists, students meet workers, managers meet globetrotters, and all enjoy the beer of the Hofbräu brewery in peace and harmony.

‹ Die Surfer am Eisbach zählen mittlerweile zu Münchens großen Touristenattraktionen – übrigens auch im Winter!

The surfers on the Eisbach have now become one of Munich's biggest tourist attractions – even in winter!

⟨ Auf dem Münchner Olympiagelände fanden 1972 die Olympischen Sommerspiele statt. Heute ist die großzügig gestaltete Grünanlage mit ihrer kühnen Zeltdachkonstruktion rund um den 291 Meter hohen Fernsehturm ein beliebtes Freizeitgelände.

The 1972 Olympic Games were held in Munich's Olympic park. Today the spacious site with its distinctive tent roofed pavillon and 291–metre TV tower, is a popular place for recreation.

⌃ Mit der BMW-Welt schufen die Münchner Autobauer nicht nur ein sehr extravagantes Auslieferungszentrum für ihre Edelkarossen, sondern auch ein architektonisches Ausrufezeichen gegenüber dem Olympiagelände.

With BMW-Welt the Munich car maker has not only created an extraordinary delivery centre for its high-class vehicles, but also an architectural exclamation mark opposite the Olympic park.

⌃ Das renommierte Architektenbüro Herzog & de Meuron entwarf die spektakuläre Fußballarena der beiden Münchner Vereine Bayern München und TSV 1860 München. Je nachdem, wer darin spielt, leuchtet die Arena in den Vereinsfarben rot oder blau.

The renowned architects' practice Herzog & de Meuron designed the spectacular football stadium for Munich's two clubs, Bayern München and TSV 1860 München. The arena is illuminated in red or blue, depending on which team is playing.

Oberbayern
Upper Bavaria

Majestätische Alpengipfel, farbenfrohe Brauchtumsfeste, barocke Dorfkirchen, prunkvolle Schlösser und schattige Biergärten unter weißblauem Himmel – das alles klingt nach Klischee und ist doch verblüffende Realität in Oberbayern. Die Donau im Norden und die Alpenkette im Süden, die Salzach im Osten und der Lech im Westen rahmen eine faszinierende Landschaft ein, in der bunte Bauernstädtchen, stille Klöster und die romantischen Schlösser König Ludwigs II. von der reichen Geschichte und Kultur der Region erzählen. Trotz der rasanten Entwicklung zum modernen Technologiestandort hat Oberbayern seine ländliche Prägung bewahrt. Und seine sprichwörtliche Gemütlichkeit, ob am vornehmen Tegernsee, im mit Lüftlbildern geschmückten Mittenwald oder auf der weit in den Himmel ragenden Zugspitze.

Majestic Alpine peaks, lively folklore festivals, Baroque village churches, magnificent palaces and shady beer gardens beneath skies of white and blue, the traditional colours of the region – what sounds like a cliché is astonishingly real in Upper Bavaria. The Danube to the north and the Alps to the south, the river Salzach to the east and the Lech to the west frame a fascinating landscape where rustic towns, peaceful monasteries and the romantic castles of King Ludwig II tell of Bavaria's historical and cultural riches. Although it has grown into a high-technology region, Upper Bavaria has kept its rural character – as well as its proverbial warm-heartedness, whether on high-class Tegernsee, in Mittenwald with its decorative façades, or at Germany's highest mountain, the Zugspitze.

Schroffer Fels über bunten Almwiesen – › dieses Panorama findet sich vielerorts in Oberbayern, so auch hier beim Blick vom Kreuzjoch auf Zug- und Alpspitze.

A rugged peak above colourful Alpine meadows – panoramas like this view from the Kreuzjoch to the Zugspitze and Alpspitze can be admired in many places in Upper Bavaria.

‹ Über Burghausen an der Salzach thront seit dem 11. Jh. eine mächtige Festung. Mit sechs hintereinander gelegenen Höfen und einer Länge von 1051 Metern gilt sie laut Guinnessbuch der Rekorde als »längste Burg der Welt«.

A fortress has perched majestically above Burghausen an der Salzach since the 11th century. With six courtyards situated one behind the other and a length of 1051 metres, it is named in the Guinness Book of Records as the »longest castle in the world«.

^ Eine Schwarze Madonna von 1330 ist Mittelpunkt der Verehrung im Wallfahrtsort Altötting, wo es selten so still wie auf diesem Winterbild ist.

A black Madonna dating from 1330 is venerated in Altötting, a place of pilgrimage that is seldom as quiet as in this winter scene.

Die Wallfahrtskirche Maria Himmelfahrt ›
oberhalb von Ramsau stammt aus dem
18. Jahrhundert.

The pilgrimage church of Maria Himmelfahrt above Ramsau dates from the 18th
century.

Die Riesenräder im Hauptbrunnenhaus der ›
Alten Saline in Bad Reichenhall treiben
neun Pumpen an, mit denen salzhaltiges
Wasser aus 15 Metern Tiefe an die Oberflä-
che befördert wird.

The giant wheels in the main well-house of
the Alte Saline in Bad Reichenhall drive nine
pumps which raise salt water to the surface
from a depth of 15 metres.

Der Watzmann, 2713 Meter hoher Schick- »
salsberg, erhebt sich über dem Städtchen
Berchtesgaden.

The Watzmann, a daunting 2713–metre
mountain, rises above the little town of
Berchtesgaden.

‹ Im südöstlichsten Winkel Oberbayerns schippern Ausflügler gern über den blau schimmernden Königssee und lauschen dem berühmten ›Trompeten-Echo‹. Bergsteiger finden mit Watzmann, dem Steinernen Meer und dem Hagengebirge eine anspruchsvolle Wanderregion vor, die als Nationalpark Berchtesgaden unter strengem Naturschutz steht.

In the furthermost south-eastern corner of Upper Bavaria, visitors enjoy excursions by boat across the shimmering blue Königssee and listen to the famous ›trumpet‹ echo. The Watzmann, Steinernes Meer and Hagengebirge offer hikers a challenging walking region where nature is strictly protected as part of the Berchtesgaden National Park.

Alpine Architektur am Berchtesgadener ›
Markt: Typisch sind die auf nassen Putz auf-
getragenen Lüftlbilder.

Alpine architecture on the marketplace in
Berchtesgaden featuring the »Lüftlbilder«,
open-air paintings created on wet plaster.

Auf der Fraueninsel im Chiemsee führen »
Schwestern vom Benediktinerorden ein
zurückgezogenes Klosterleben.

On the Fraueninsel (women's island) in
Chiemsee, sisters of the Benedictine order
live in their monastic retreat.

Im Schutz der Innschleife entwickelte sich ›
Wasserburg zwischen dem 13. und dem
17. Jahrhundert zu einem bedeutenden
Handelsumschlagsplatz für Salz.

Protected on its loop in the river Inn, Wasserburg developed into an important trading place for salt between the 13th and
17th centuries.

Auch Rosenheim lebte jahrhundertelang ›
vom Handel mit Salz.

Rosenheim also lived from the salt trade for
centuries.

Von der Kampenwand schweift der Blick »
ungehindert über das fruchtbare Voralpen-
land rund um den Chiemsee.

From the Kampenwand there is an uninter-
rupted view of the fertile Alpine foothills
around the lake Chiemsee.

Die Ausstattung des Doms zu Freising ›
stammt aus der Blütezeit des Rokoko und
ist eine Arbeit der genialen Brüder Cosmas
Damian und Egid Quirin Asam.

The interior of Freising Cathedral dates
from the golden age of Rococo art, and was
the work of the brilliant brothers Cosmas
Damian and Egid Quirin Asam.

In Neuburg an der Donau steht eines der ›
wenigen erhaltenen Renaissanceschlösser
in Oberbayern.

Neuburg an der Donau is the site of one of
the few surviving Renaissance palaces in
Upper Bavaria.

Besinnung im schlicht-schönen Kreuzgang ›
des Doms zu Eichstätt aus dem 13./14. Jahrhundert.

Tranquillity in the simple beauty of the
13th and 14th century cloisters of Eichstätt
Cathedral.

Das Ingolstädter Kreuztor aus dem 14. Jahr- »
hundert wendet der Altstadt seine schlich-
tere Fassade zu.

The 14th century Kreuztor gate in Ingol-
stadt presents its plainer façade to the old
town.

‹ Landsberg am Lech verleiht der über mehrere Stufen strömende Lech ein besonderes Flair. Die alten Stadtviertel am Fluss sind heute noch von den ehemaligen Warenspeichern, den Stadln, geprägt.

The weir on the river Lech in Landsberg am Lech gives the town a special flair. The old quarters by the river are still marked by Stadln, buildings which were once used as warehouses.

‹ Über dem Ostufer des Ammersees liegt mit dem Kloster Andechs der älteste Wallfahrtsort Bayerns. Berühmt ist auch das klostereigene Andechser Bier.

Above the east bank of Ammersee lies Kloster Andechs, the oldest place of pilgrimage in Bavaria. The monastery's own Andechser beer is also famous.

« Das außen eher schlichte Dießener Marienmünster aus dem 18. Jahrhundert prunkt innen mit üppigem Barock- und Rokokoschmuck.

The 18th century Marienmünster in Diessen, plain from the outside, has an opulently decorated Baroque and Rococo interior.

Südlich des Starnberger Sees bilden die ⌃ Osterseen smaragdgrüne Tupfer in einer stillen Moorlandschaft.

South of Starnberger See, the lakes known as the Osterseen add spots of emerald green to a quiet moor landscape.

Weißwurst, Brezen, Weißbier, dazu süßer ⟩ Senf – so sieht eine typische Brotzeit in einem Starnberger Biergarten aus.

Wheat beer, pretzels and white sausage seasoned with sweet mustard – a typical pre-lunch snack in a beer garden in Starnberg.

Im Hochsommer bleibt auf den Stegen und ⬆ an den Stränden des Starnberger Sees kaum ein Plätzchen frei.

At the height of summer there is hardly a free space on the jetties and beaches of Starnberger See.

Oberbayerisches Brauchtum wird gepflegt, ⌃
so auch die farbenfrohe Leonhardifahrt in
Bad Tölz.

In Upper Bavaria traditions are maintained,
for example the colourful Leonhardifahrt in
Bad Tölz.

Fotogen schmiegt sich der auch bei Promi- ⟩
nenten sehr beliebte Tegernsee zwischen
die Voralpengipfel.

Tegernsee, a lake beloved of celebrities,
nestles prettily between the summits of
Alpine foothills.

Halsbrecherisch sind die traditionellen ⌃
Hornschlittenrennen in Gaißach.

The traditional horn-sledge races in
Gaissach are run at breakneck pace.

‹ In diesem hübschen Haus in Murnau lebte die Malerin Gabriele Münter mit ihrem Lebensgefährten Wassily Kandinsky von 1909 bis 1914.

The painter Gabriele Münter lived in this pretty house in Murnau with her partner, Vassily Kandinsky, from 1909 to 1914.

⌃ Nur an wenigen Stellen ist der Staffelsee öffentlich zugänglich. Der größte Teil steht unter Naturschutz oder ist privaten Anrainern vorbehalten.

The shore of Staffelsee is accessible to the public only in a few places. Most of it is a protected nature reserve or privately owned by residents.

⌃ Im Freilichtmuseum Glentleiten werden in alten Bauernhöfen, Ställen und Schmieden die Lebens- und Arbeitsbedingungen des 18. und 19. Jahrhunderts wachgehalten.

In the open-air museum at Glentleiten, the conditions of life and work in the 18th and 19th centuries are kept alive in old farmyards, animal stalls and smithies.

⟨ Herbststimmung am Kochelsee. Die Maler der Künstlergruppe Blauer Reiter liebten die weichen Farben und immer neuen Perspektiven ihrer Wahlheimat am Fuß des 1731 Meter hohen Herzogstands.

Autumn mood on Kochelsee. The Blauer Reiter Group of artists loved the soft colours and constantly changing perspectives of the place where they chose to live at the foot of the 1731-metre-high Herzogstand.

⋩ Das Rißtal gilt als eines der schönsten Alpentäler Oberbayerns.

The Risstal is one of the most beautiful Alpine valleys of Upper Bavaria.

⌃ Wallgau im Werdenfelser Land liegt nahe der österreichischen Grenze und verfügt über ein gutes Loipennetz.

Wallgau in the Werdenfelser Land lies close to the Austrian border and has a good network of tracks for cross-country skiing.

Die im Pfaffenwinkel beheimatete Wies- › kirche wurde Mitte des 18. Jahrhunderts im Rokokostil erbaut. Sie ist heute Unesco-Welterbe.

The Wieskirche, a church in the Pfaffenwinkel built in the mid-18th century in the Rococo style, is a listed Unesco World Heritage site.

Das einzige Schloss, dessen Vollendung » Bauherr König Ludwig II. noch miterleben durfte – Schloss Linderhof mit seinem weitläufigen Landschaftsgarten.

The only palace that King Ludwig II commissioned and lived to see completed: Linderhof Palace with its extensive landscaped garden.

Auf dem Kuppelfresko in der Basilika des › Klosters Ettal fügen sich über 400 Einzelfiguren zu einem himmlischen Tableau.

On the fresco beneath the dome of the basilica of Ettal monastery, 400 individual figures combine to form a heavenly tableau.

Ludwig II. war Fan einer überbordenden » Innenausstattung – hier der Spiegelsaal in Schloss Linderhof.

Ludwig II loved exuberant interiors – here the Hall of Mirrors in Linderhof Palace.

Oberammergau gilt als Dorf mit den »
schönsten Lüftlmalereien Oberbayerns.
Diese Technik des Fassadenschmucks soll
hier erfunden worden sein.

The outdoor paintings in Oberammergau
are regarded as the most beautiful in Upper
Bavaria. This technique of decorating
façades is said to have been invented here.

Auch im modernen und geschäftigen Gar- »
misch-Partenkirchen gibt es noch einige
Straßen, die dem oberbayerischen Dorf-
ideal entsprechen.

Even busy, modern Garmisch-Partenkirchen has a few streets that match the
Upper Bavarian ideal of a perfect village.

Ein Wanderweg führt winters wie sommers ›
durch die 900 Meter lange Partnachklamm
bei Garmisch-Partenkirchen.

In winter as in summer, a walking trail passes
through the 900-metre-long Partnachklamm ravine near Garmisch-Partenkirchen.

Die sanften Wellen der Buckelwiesen bei ⌃
Mittenwald kontrastieren mit den schroffen
Felswänden des Karwendelgebirges.

Gentle undulations of the »bumpy meadows«
near Mittenwald contrast with the rugged
rock walls of the Karwendel Mountains.

∧ Das Riesenfernrohr auf der Karwendelspitze erlaubt einen spektakulären Blick in den 1000 Meter tiefen Abgrund.

The giant telescope on the Karwendelspitze provides a spectacular view, 1000 metres down into the abyss.

Allgäu & Schwaben
Allgau & Swabia

Zwischen Bodensee und Lech erstreckt sich eine Region mit vielen Gesichtern: Im Süden bildet das Allgäu mit schroffen Berggipfeln, sattgrünen Almwiesen und alten Bauerndörfern die Grenze zu Österreich. Wildbäche rauschen durch malerische Schluchten und im Brauchtum lebt heidnischer Glauben weiter. Historische Städtchen wie Kempten oder Kaufbeuren schmücken Bauten vom Mittelalter bis zur Renaissance, während Kirchen und Klöster das Loblied des üppigen Barock singen. In Augsburg begegnet man der Weltläufigkeit und dem Reichtum einer Kaufmannsfamilie: Die Fugger haben die Stadt architektonisch, kulturell wie gesellschaftlich geprägt. Ganz im Westen bildet Lindau eine bayerische Enklave am Bodensee: Wahrzeichen der charmanten Stadt ist ein mächtiger bayerischer Löwe an der Hafeneinfahrt.

The land between Lake Constance and the river Lech has many faces. To the south, the Allgau with its rugged mountain peaks, lush green alpine meadows and old rustic villages forms the border with Austria. Wild mountain streams rush through picturesque gorges, and pagan beliefs survive in the local customs. Buildings from the Middle Ages and Renaissance adorn historic towns like Kempten and Kaufbeuren, while churches and monasteries sing God's praises in extravagant Baroque style. Visitors to Augsburg encounter a wealthy and cosmopolitan merchant family: the Fuggers, who put their stamp on the architecture, culture and society of the city. In the far west, Lindau is a Bavarian enclave on Lake Constance: the emblem of this charming town is a proud Bavarian lion at the harbour entrance.

Oberstaufen-Steibis liegt mit seinen Weilern und dem Alpgebiet im Naturpark Nagelfluhkette mit dem Hochgrat. ›

Oberstaufen-Steibis with its hamlets and alpine landscape is situated in the Nagelfluhkette Nature Park beneath the Hochgrat.

In Bad Wörishofen wird die von Sebastian »
Kneipp entwickelte Kur gepflegt. 1855 kam
der Pfarrer als Beichtvater für die Benedik-
tinerinnen in das Dorf und begann schon
bald, mit der heilenden Kraft von Wasser zu
experimentieren.

A health cure developed by Sebastian
Kneipp is practised in Bad Wörishofen. In
1855 he came to the village as a father con-
fessor for Benedictine nuns and soon be-
gan to experiment with the healing powers
of water.

Mitte des 19. Jahrhunderts erhielt die Studi- »
enkirche Maria Himmelfahrt in Dillingen ihr
strahlendes Rokokogewand.

In the mid-19th century the college church
of Maria Himmelfahrt in Dillingen was decorated with radiant white Rococo ornamen-
tation.

Nördlingen ist von einer knapp drei Kilome- ›
ter langen mittelalterlichen Stadtmauer
umgeben. Einzigartig in Deutschland ist
der vollständig erhaltene überdachte
Wehrgang.

Nördlingen is surrounded by a medieval
town wall almost three kilometres long.
The completely intact battlement roofing is
unique in Germany.

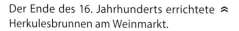

In Augsburg am Lech verbinden sich male- ⚌
rische Lage, intakte Altstadt und entspann-
ter Lebensstil.

Augsburg on the river Lech is a combinati-
on of picturesque location, an intact old
town and a relaxed lifestyle.

Mitte des 14. Jahrhunderts entstand das ⌃
prunkvolle gotische Südportal des Augsburger Doms.

The magnificent south doorway of Augsburg Cathedral dates from the mid-14th
century.

Der Ende des 16. Jahrhunderts errichtete ⚌
Herkulesbrunnen am Weinmarkt.

The Hercules Fountain on Weinmarkt, built
in the late 16th century.

Die 1521 gestiftete Fuggerei gilt als älteste ⌃
noch erhaltene Sozialsiedlung der Welt.

The Fuggerei of 1521 is thought to be the
world's oldest surviving social housing.

Das Augsburger Renaissance-Rathaus war ⟩
stolzer Ausdruck wirtschaftlicher Macht.

Augsburg's Renaissance town hall was a
proud expression of economic power.

Im romantischen Städtchen Babenhausen ›
herrschte ab dem 16. Jahrhundert ein
Zweig der Augsburger Fuggerfamilie. Erst
1806 endete die Fürstenherrschaft und es
wurde dem Königreich Bayern zugeschla-
gen.

A branch of the Fugger family from Augsburg ruled the romantic little town of Babenhausen from the late 16th century.
Their rule did not end until 1806, when the
principality was merged with the Kingdom
of Bavaria.

Bei den alle vier Jahre stattfindenden Wal- ›
lensteinfestspielen gibt das Steuerhaus in
Memmingen eine perfekte historische Ku-
lisse für den nachgespielten Einmarsch von
Wallensteins Truppen im Jahr 1630 ab.

In the Wallensteinfestspiele, a festival held
every four years, the Steuerhaus in Memmingen is the perfect historical backdrop
for a re-enactment of the entrance of
Wallenstein's soldiers in 1630.

‹ Als die Basilika St. Alexander und St. Theodor des Klosters Ottobeuren im 18. Jahrhundert erbaut wurde, war die Creme de la creme der Barockbaumeister, u. a. die Brüder Zeiller und Johann Michael Fischer, daran beteiligt.

When the Basilica of St Alexander and St Theodor at the monastery in Ottobeuren was built in the 18th century, the crème de la crème of Baroque architects, for example the Zeiller brothers and Johann Michael Fischer, played their part.

‹ Seit mehr als fünf Jahrhunderten ist das Tänzelfest in der historischen Altstadt von Kaufbeuren verbrieft. In Umzügen lassen Kinder und Jugendliche die Geschichte der Stadt lebendig werden.

The Tänzelfest in the old quarter of Kaufbeuren is known to be more than 500 years old. Processions of children and young people bring the history of the town to life.

Auf dem Fellhorn bei Oberstdorf stimmen ≫
sich die Alphornbläser für ein Ständchen in
luftiger Höhe ein.

On the Fellhorn near Oberstdorf, Alphorn
players prepare to make music up on the
mountain.

Zum Viehscheid im Herbst werden die ^
Kühe hinunter ins Tal getrieben.

In autumn the cattle are driven down into
the valley from the Alpine meadows.

Scheideggs St.-Hubertus-Kapelle ist das ›
einzige ökumenische Gotteshaus im Allgäu. Errichtet wurde es erst in den 1980er-
Jahren.

The Chapel of St Hubertus in Scheidegg is
the only ecumenical place of worship in
Allgau. It was built in the 1980s.

‹ Die spektakulärsten Schlösser verdankt Bayern Ludwig II. Die Fertigstellung von Neuschwanstein, das heute wirkt wie eine Walt-Disney-Kopie (tatsächlich ist es umgekehrt), erlebte der versponnene König nicht mehr.

The most stunning Bavarian palaces were the work of Ludwig II. The eccentric monarch did not live to see the completion of Neuschwanstein, which today seems like an imitation of a Walt Disney castle – but in fact it is the other way round.

˄ Einem byzantinischen Gotteshaus sollte der Thronsaal gleichen – Ludwig II. sah sich als von göttlicher Gnade eingesetzter, absoluter Fürst und stattete seine Schlösser mit den Symbolen dieser imaginären Macht aus.

The Throne Room was intended to look like a Byzantine church: Ludwig II saw himself as an absolute ruler by divine right and installed symbols of this imaginary power in his palaces.

‹ König Maximilian II., Vater Ludwigs II., ließ die seit dem 12. Jahrhundert bezeugte Burg Hohenschwangau um 1837 neugotisch um- und aufbauen.

In about 1837 King Maximilian II, the father of Ludwig II, had the 12th century Hohenschwangau Castle rebuilt and extended in the neo-Gothic style.

« Füssen: Blick über die Barockanlage des ehemaligen Benediktinerklosters St. Mang, den Lech und die Füssener Enge, durch die im Mittelalter ein Fernhandelsweg verlief.

Füssen: View of the baroque buildings of the former Benedictine monastery of St Mang, the river Lech and the Füssen Gap. A trade route passed through here in the Middle Ages.

‹ Der markante Gipfel des 2592 Meter hohen Hochvogels ist das Ziel einer reizvollen Wanderung von Bad Hindelang.

The striking peak of the 2592–metre Hochvogel lies at the end of an enjoyable walk from Bad Hindelang.

« Kloster St. Mang in Füssen liegt am Lech, darüber erhebt sich das gotische Hohe Schloss, die ehemalige Sommerresidenz der Fürstbischöfe von Augsburg.

The monastery of St Mang in Füssen is situated on the banks of the river Lech, the gothic »Hohe Schloss«, the former summer residence of the prince bishops of Augsburg, towers above.

Das auf 800 Meter gelegene Oberstdorf » liegt geschützt zwischen Berggipfeln in einem von der Sonne verwöhnten Kessel. Markantester Berg über dem Ort ist das 2224 m hohe Nebelhorn.

At a height of 800 metres, Oberstdorf enjoys a sheltered location in a sunny valley between the mountain peaks. The highest is the 2224–metre Nebelhorn.

Nicht weit von Oberstdorf hat sich die » Breitach eine bis zu 100 Meter tiefe, wildromantische Klamm in den Fels gegraben.

Close to Oberstdorf the river Breitach has carved a wild and romantic 100-metre-deep ravine out of the rock.

Das Nebelhorn bietet Wanderern Tourenmöglichkeiten aller Schwierigkeitsgrade, darunter auch den Einstieg zum Hindelanger Klettersteig.

Hikers can enjoy walks of varying levels of difficulty on the Nebelhorn, including the approach to the via ferrata of Hindelang.

‹ Mit der 1972 in Betrieb genommenen Hochgratbahn schweben die Fahrgäste auf den 1834 Meter hohen Hausberg von Oberstaufen.

On the Hochgratbahn, which opened in 1972, passengers glide up to the 1834-metre-high mountain behind Oberstaufen.

≈ Der Große Alpsee bei Immenstadt ist Teil des Naturparks Nagelfluhkette und wegen seines Fischreichtums Ziel vieler Angler.

The Grosser Alpsee near Immenstadt is part of the Nagelfluhkette nature park and a destination for many anglers.

⌃ Das Kemptener Rathaus aus dem 15. und 16. Jahrhundert dominiert den Marktplatz.

The 15th and 16th century town hall of Kempten dominates the marketplace.

Lindau liegt nicht am, sondern im Boden- ›
see, denn die Altstadt ist eine mit dem Fest-
land verbundene Insel. In der Maximilians-
straße sind viele prachtvolle Hausfassaden
von Gotik bis Barock erhalten. Charakteristisch sind die Brodlauben, Spitzbogenarka-
den, unter denen Brot verkauft wurde.

Lindau lies not on, but in Lake Constance,
as its old town is an island joined to the
mainland. In Maximiliansstrasse many superb house façades from the Gothic to Baroque periods have survived. A characteristic feature are the Brodlauben, arcades with
pointed arches beneath which bread was
sold.

Das Haus zum Cavazzen, heute Stadtmuse- ›
um, wurde 1729 mit doppelstöckigem
Walmdach und reichem Freskenschmuck
erbaut.

The Haus zum Cavazzen, now the town museum, was built in 1729 with a two-storey
hipped roof and opulent frescoes.

Der Löwe in der Hafeneinfahrt von Lindau »
signalisiert ankommenden Schiffen, dass
sie hier an bayerischem Boden anlanden.

The lion at the entrance to the harbour of
Lindau is a signal to approaching ships that
they will land on Bavarian soil here.

Franken
Franconia

Bayerns nördliche Region glänzt mit vier Unesco-Welterbestätten: der Altstadt von Bamberg, beispielhaft für die mittelalterliche Entwicklung einer Stadt, der Fürstbischöflichen Residenz zu Würzburg, einem Meisterwerk des Barock, dem markgräflichen Opernhaus in Bayreuth als einzigem im Original erhaltenen Opernhaus dieser Epoche, und dem Limes, der nur als Bodendenkmal zu erahnen ist. Frankens Metropole Nürnberg war Kaiserresidenz und Handelsstadt – der damalige Wohlstand spiegelt sich in der historischen Altstadt. Mit den unter Naturschutz stehenden Mittelgebirgslandschaften des Fichtelgebirges und des Spessarts bezaubert Franken auch Naturfreunde. Weinliebhaber kommen angesichts der dicht mit Reben bestandenen Hänge im Maintal ins Schwärmen. Romantischer Höhepunkt ist jedoch das Fachwerkstädtchen Rothenburg ob der Tauber.

Bavaria's northern province boasts four Unesco World Heritage sites: the old town of Bamberg, a fine example of urban development in the Middle Ages; the prince electors' residence in Würzburg, a Baroque masterpiece; the margraves' opera house in Bayreuth, the only one from this era to be preserved in its original condition; and the Limes, the Roman border which survives only as archaeological remains. Nuremberg, the leading Franconian city, was a trading centre and residence for emperors, sources of wealth which are still reflected in its historic quarter. With the protected hilly landscape of the Fichtelgebirge and Spessart, Franconia also has treats for nature lovers, while the slopes of the Main valley, densely covered in vines, delight wine enthusiasts. The romantic highlight of the region is the half-timbered town of Rothenburg ob der Tauber.

Seit dem 12. Jahrhundert beherrscht die › mächtige Höhenburg als nördlichste Burg Bayerns das oberfränkische Lauenstein.

Since the 12th century the mighty Höhenburg, Bavaria's northernmost castle, has loomed above Lauenstein in Upper Franconia.

« Nur noch wenige historische Bauten erinnern in der Altstadt von Hof an die lange Geschichte der Siedlung an der Saale.

Only a few historic buildings remain in Hof's old town. They now serve as reminders of the long history of this town on the river Saale.

« Bayreuths Opernhaus zählt als eines der wenigen erhaltenen Theater aus der Barockzeit seit 2012 zum Unesco-Welterbe.

Bayreuth's opera house, one of a small number of surviving theatres from the Baroque period, has been a Unesco World Heritage site since 2012.

« Die Kulmbacher Plassenburg gilt als eine der schönsten Festungen nördlich der Alpen. Ihre Schlosskapelle mit dem eleganten Eingangsportal ist ein beliebter Trauungsort.

The Plassenburg in Kulmbach is regarded as one of the most beautiful fortresses north of the Alps. The palace chapel with its elegant doorway is a popular place for weddings.

« Das Neue Rathaus von Coburg aus dem 16. Jahrhundert ist der eleganten Architektur der Renaissance verpflichtet.

The Neues Rathaus in Coburg, a 16th century town hall, was built in fine Renaissance style.

‹ Die Festung Rosenberg, eine ehemalige Burg der Bamberger Bischöfe, thront auf einem steilen Hügel über Kronach.

The fortress of Rosenberg, once a castle belonging to the bishops of Bamberg, stands majestically on a steep hill above Kronach.

Fasziniernde Tropfsteinskulpturen schmü- ⌃
cken die Teufelshöhle in der Fränkischen
Schweiz.

Fascinating dripstone sculptures adorn the
Teufelshöhle, a cave in the Fränkische
Schweiz (»Franconian Switzerland«).

Die ellipsenförmige, hochbarocke Stiftskir- ⌃
che des Klosters Banz in Bad Staffelstein
zählt zu den ungewöhnlichsten Gottes-
häusern Frankens.

The ellipse-shaped high-Baroque colle-
giate church of Banz monastery in Bad Staffelstein is one of the most unusual churches
in Franconia.

Nur der Steinerne Beutel blieb von der im ⌃
13. Jahrhundert erbauten Burg Waischenfeld.

The tower named Steinerner Beutel is all
that remains of the 13th century castle Burg
Waischenfeld.

Im 18. Jahrhundert wurde der Park Sans- ⌃
pareil zwischen Kulmbach und Bayreuth
angelegt.

Park Sanspareil between Kulmbach and
Bayreuth was laid out in the 18th century.

Basilika Vierzehnheiligen bei Bad Staffelstein. ⟩

Vierzehnheiligen Basilica, Bad Staffelstein.

« Der Legende nach wurde das Bamberger Brückenrathaus im 15. Jahrhundert auf Pfählen in den Fluss Regnitz gesetzt, weil der herrschende Fürstbischof seinen Bürgern Grund und Boden für das Bauwerk verwehrt hatte.

According to legend the town hall on the bridge in Bamberg was constructed on piles in the river Regnitz in the 15th century because the ruling prince bishop refused to give his citizens land for the building.

« Als Beispiel für eine hervorragend erhaltene mittelalterliche Stadtstruktur wurde Bamberg zum Unesco-Welterbe ernannt.

Bamberg was designated a Unesco World Heritage site as an outstanding example of a preserved medieval urban structure.

‹ Vier Türme schmücken den spätromanischen Bamberger Dom, der als Grablege des Kaisers Heinrich II. und seiner Gattin Kunigunde zu den vier deutschen Kaiserdomen zählt.

Four towers adorn the late Romanesque cathedral of Bamberg, which, as the burial place of Emperor Henry II and his wife Kunigunde, is one of Germany's four imperial cathedrals.

‹ Burg Hohenstein, die ab dem 11. Jahrhundert errichtet wurde, beherrscht die zur Fränkischen Alb zählende Hersbrucker Alb in Mittelfranken.

Hohenstein Castle, which dates back to the 11th century, dominates the Hersbrucker Alb in Middle Franconia, which is part of the Fränkische Alb hills.

≽ Über 200 000 Kirschbäume blühen im Frühjahr in der »Kirschenkammer Deutschlands« zwischen Nürnberg, Bamberg und Bayreuth.

More than 200,000 cherry trees flower in spring in »Germany's cherry orchard« between Nuremberg, Bamberg and Bayreuth.

⌃ Im Sommerhalbjahr schnauft die Dampfbahn Fränkische Schweiz an den Wochenenden durch das idyllische Wiesenttal zwischen Ebermannstadt und Behringersmühle.

On summer weekends the locomotives of the Fränkische Schweiz steam railway puff through the idyllic Wiesenttal between Ebermannstadt and Behringersmühle.

« Das Barockschloss Weißenstein oberhalb von Pommersfelden sollte seinem Erbauer, dem Bamberger Fürstbischof Lothar Franz von Schönborn, als Sommerresidenz dienen. Das ausladende und kühn konzipierte Treppenhaus war damals beispiellos.

The Baroque Weissenstein Palace above Pommersfelden was built as a summer residence for a prince bishop of Bamberg, Lothar Franz von Schönborn. The generously sized, boldly designed stairway was unprecedented in its day.

« Forchheim, die alte oberfränkische Königs- und Pfalzstadt, gilt als Eingangstor zur Fränkischen Schweiz.

Forchheim, an ancient royal and palatine town in Upper Franconia, is regarded as the gateway to the Fränkische Schweiz.

‹ Viele Male wechselte die im 12. Jahrhundert auf einem Felssporn über Wolfsberg erbaute Burg den Besitzer. Heute dient die malerische Ruine als Aussichtspunkt über dem Trubachtal.

The castle built in the 12th century on a spur of rock above Wolfsberg changed hands many times. Today the picturesque ruin is a viewing point for the Trubach Valley.

Mit den Rokoko-Festspielen erfüllt Ansbach jedes Jahr seine Markgräfliche Residenz mit Leben. ›

The margraves' residence in Ansbach is filled with life at the annual Rococo festival.

Enderndorf ist eines der vielen hübschen Städtchen im Fränkischen Seenland, einem Bade- und Freizeitparadies aus mehreren aufgestauten Seen. »

Enderndorf is one of many pretty little towns in the Fränkisches Seenland, a paradise for swimming and leisure activities consisting of several artificial lakes.

An der Nordwestecke der Dinkelsbühler Stadtmauer erinnern Faulturm und Zwinger an die mittelalterliche Gerichtsbarkeit. ›

At the north-west corner of the town wall of Dinkelsbühl, the Faulturm and Zwinger are reminders of judicial powers in the Middle Ages.

Um 1700 begannen die Arbeiten am Markgräflichen Schloss Erlangen, das heute Sitz der Universitätsverwaltung ist. »

Work on the margraves' palace in Erlangen, today seat of the university administration, started around the year 1700.

Zwischen 1509 und 1528 lebte und arbeitete der Maler Albrecht Dürer in diesem Fachwerkhaus in der Nürnberger Altstadt, das heute als Museum dient. ›

Between 1509 and 1528 the painter Albrecht Dürer lived in the old town of Nuremberg in this half-timbered house, which is now a museum.

Alt und Neu kontrastieren beim Nürnberger Stadttheater auf spannende Weise miteinander: Das klassizistische Opernhaus wurde zu Beginn des 20. Jahrhunderts errichtet, das Schauspielhaus gegenüber 1959 eröffnet und Anfang des 21. Jahrhunderts generalsaniert. ›

Old and new form an exciting contrast at Nuremberg's municipal theatre: the neoclassical opera house was built in the early 20th century, while the theatre opposite opened in 1959 and was thoroughly renovated in the early 21st century.

Nürnbergs Kaiserburg mit dem runden Sinwellturm hat Wurzeln, die bis ins 12. Jahrhundert und zur Herrschaft der Staufer zurückreichen. ›

Nuremberg's Kaiserburg with its round Sinwellturm is a castle that goes back to the 12th century and the rule of the Staufer dynasty.

Weltberühmt ist der Nürnberger Christkindlesmarkt, der traditionell von einem als Christkind verkleideten Mädchen eröffnet wird. »

Nuremberg's Christkindlesmarkt, which is traditionally opened by a girl dressed as the Baby Jesus, is world-famous.

‹ Balthasar Neumann, Erbauer der Würzburger Residenz, zeichnete auch für den Bau des Barockschlosses Werneck unweit von Schweinfurt verantwortlich.

Balthasar Neumann, architect of Würzburg Palace, was also responsible for building the Baroque palace at Werneck near Schweinfurt.

‹ Ochsenfurts Altstadt ist ein romantisches, historisches Ensemble mit schmalen, mittelalterlichen Gassen und Fachwerkhäusern mit vorkragendem Obergeschoss.

The old quarter of Ochsenfurt is a romantic, historic ensemble of narrow medieval alleys and half-timbered houses with projecting upper storeys.

« Der klassizistische, von Max Littmann zu Beginn des 20. Jahrhunderts errichtete Regentenbau mit seiner eleganten Gartenanlage ist Bad Kissingens Wahrzeichen.

The neoclassical Regentenbau, built by Max Littmann in the early 20th century with its lovely gardens, is the emblem of Bad Kissingen.

‹ Der Blick von der Würzburger Altstadt über die Alte Mainbrücke auf die Renaissancefeste Marienberg zählt zu den reizvollsten Perspektiven der Mainmetropole.

The view from Würzburg's old town across the old Main bridge (Alte Mainbrücke) to the Renaissance fortress of Marienberg is one of the city's most pleasing prospects.

‹ Größte Attraktion des Barockschlosses von Veitshöchheim ist der zauberhafte Rokokogarten.

The greatest attraction of the Baroque palace of Veitshöchheim is its enchanting Rococo garden.

‹ Fachwerk und Weinreben prägen Homburg am Main.

Homburg am Main is a place of half-timbered houses and vines.

« Grandioses Entrée: Die von Balthasar Neumann und Giovanni Battista Tiepolo gestaltete Barocktreppe der Würzburger Residenz.

A magnificent entrance: the Baroque stairway of Würzburg Palace, the work of Balthasar Neumann and Giovanni Battista Tiepolo.

Das Renaissanceschloss Johannesburg in ⌃ Aschaffenburg zeigt eine interessante Sammlung von Modellen antiker Bauten.

The Renaissance Johannesburg Palace in Aschaffenburg boasts an interesting collection of models of ancient buildings.

Märchenhaft wirkt das Wasserschloss ⌃ Mespelbrunn im Spessart.

The moated castle of Mespelbrunn in the Spessart area has a fairy-tale quality.

Ein Parade-Fachwerkstädtchen ist Milten- ❯ berg zwischen Mainknie und den Hängen von Odenwald und Spessart.

Miltenberg between the »Main knee« and the slopes of the Odenwald and Spessart is a charming half-timbered little town.

In der Abteikirche des Klosters Amorbach ❯❯ ist eine wertvolle Barockorgel erhalten.

A precious Baroque organ has survived in the abbey church of Amorbach monastery.

‹ Rothenburg ob der Tauber zieht mit seiner nahezu intakt erhaltenen mittelalterlichen Altstadt, die von einem Mauergürtel mit mehr als 40 Türmen umgeben ist, jedes Jahr Millionen von Touristen an.

With its almost completely intact medieval old quarter, surrounded by walls with over 40 towers, Rothenburg ob der Tauber attracts millions of tourists every year.

Niederbayern & Oberpfalz
Lower Bavaria & Upper Palatinate

Stille Schönheit gibt es im östlichen Bayern zu entdecken: Die von der Mittelgebirgslandschaft des Bayerischen und des Oberpfälzer Waldes geprägte Grenzregion zu Tschechien stand lange abseits des touristischen Interesses und blieb dadurch unverfälscht, fast herb. Dunkle Wälder, geheimnisvolle Bergseen und aussichtsreiche Berggipfel begleiten die Donau, an der historische Städte wie das ländliche Straubing oder das fürstbischöfliche Passau residieren. Zum Unesco-Welterbe zählt die bestens erhaltene Altstadt von Regensburg mit ihren Kaufmannstürmen, dem einzigartigen Dom und der Steinernen Brücke – Wunderwerke mittelalterlicher Baukunst. Bei Kelheim, wo die Donau eine Felsbarriere durchbricht, verbirgt sich hinter Klostermauern ein hochbarockes Gotteshaus in jubilierender Vollendung.

Tranquil beauty awaits discovery in the east of Bavaria: the region on the border of the Czech Republic, the hilly woodland of the Bayerischer Wald and the Oberpfälzer Wald, lay off the tourist track for a long time, and thus retained its authentic, almost stark character. Dark forests, mysterious highland lakes and mountain summits with magnificent views accompany the Danube on its course through historic towns such as rural Straubing and Passau, the seat of prince-bishops. The extremely well-preserved old town of Regensburg with its merchants' towers, unique cathedral and ancient stone bridge – miracles of medieval architecture – is a Unesco World Heritage site. At Kelheim, where the Danube breaks through a rocky barrier, a church in exuberant high-Baroque style lies behind monastery walls.

Weit reicht der Blick vom Großen Arber › über die verschneite Mittelgebirgslandschaft des Oberpfälzer Waldes.

From the Grosser Arber, the view ranges far over the snowy landscape of the Mittelgebirge uplands in the Upper Palatinate Forest.

« »Natur Natur sein lassen« lautet das Motto des Nationalparks Bayerischer Wald – so wie hier in der Umgebung des Watzlik-Hains.

Let nature be nature – this is the motto of the Bavarian Forest National Park, as can be seen here near the Watzlik Woods.

⌃ Im Freigelände des Nationalparkzentrums Falkenstein bekommen Besucher einen Eindruck davon, wie der scheue Wolf lebt.

On the grounds of the national park centre in Falkenstein visitors can get an impression of how wolves live.

⌃ Der Große Arbersee an der Flanke des namengebenden Berges ist ein Relikt der letzten Eiszeit.

Grosser Arbersee on the flank of the mountain from which it takes its name is a relic of the last Ice Age.

« Über 150 Originalbauten vom 16. bis zum 19. Jahrhundert hat ein Unternehmer im Museumsdorf Bayerischer Wald nahe Tittling wieder aufbauen lassen. Dem »Dorf« hauchen Schmiede, Schnitzer, Bauern und Bäcker echtes Leben ein.

More than 150 original buildings from the 16th to the 19th century have been re-erected by a businessman in the museum village of the Bavarian Forest near Tittling. A smithy, carvers, farmers and bakers bring a touch of real life to the »village«.

« Riedlhütte ist einer der vielen Glashüttenorte im Bayerischen Wald, wo seit Jahrhunderten mundgeblasenes Glas hergestellt wird – Liebhaber wissen es zu schätzen.

Riedlhütte is one of many centres of glassmaking in the Bavarian Forest, where mouth-blown glass has been made for centuries – to the delight of connoisseurs.

‹ Wer den 1312 Meter hohen Dreisessel bestiegen hat, genießt eine herrliche Fernsicht über Bayerischen und Böhmerwald.

The reward for climbing the 1312–metre Dreisessel is a superb view across the Bavarian and Bohemian Forest.

Von der Veste Oberhaus regierten die ≫
Passauer Fürstbischöfe ihre Stadt.

From Veste Oberhaus the prince bishops of
Passau ruled the city.

Italienische Barockarchitektur lässt die ⌃
Fassade des Passauer Doms St. Stephan
schwingen.

Italian Baroque architecture puts curves
in the façade of St Stephen's Cathedral in
Passau.

Das Passauer Dreiflüsseeck aus der Vogel- ›
perspektive: Hier verstärken der von Süden
heranströmende, hellgrüne Inn und die
dunklen Wasser der Ilz von Norden den
breiten mittleren Lauf der Donau.

A bird's-eye view of the confluence of three
rivers at Passau: here the light green Inn
flowing from the south and the dark waters
of the Ilz from the north swell the broad
middle section of the Danube.

⌐ Der Kötztinger Pfingstritt startet am Pfingstmontag in Bad Kötzting und führt durchs Zellertal in das sieben Kilometer entfernte Steinbühl, wo die Pferde an der Kirche St. Nikolaus feierlich gesegnet werden.

The Kötztinger Pfingstritt, a ride on Whit Monday, leads seven kilometres from Bad Kötzting through the Zellertal valley to Steinbühl, where the horses are ceremoniously blessed at St Nicholas' Church.

‹ Der Schwarze Regen ist beliebt für Kanuwanderungen. Meist strömt er ruhig durch die stille Landschaft des Vorwaldes und passiert dabei Städtchen wie Regen mit der markanten Pfarrkirche St. Michael.

The Schwarze Regen is a popular river for canoe tours. Usually it flows gently through the quiet countryside of the Vorwald, passing through little towns such as Regen with its eye-catching St Michael's Church.

⌃ Das Straubinger Gäubodenfest ist nach Meinung Vieler das reizvollste Volksfest Bayerns und dem Münchner Oktoberfest durch seine Bodenständigkeit und das Traditionsbewusstsein seiner Besucher weit überlegen.

The Gäubodenfest in Straubing is said by many to be the most enjoyable fair in Bavaria, and far superior to the Oktoberfest in Munich thanks to its down-to-earth character and traditionally-minded visitors.

Die barocke Ausstattung der kleinen Wall- ⌃
fahrtskirche Weißenregen ist ungewöhnlich
qualitätvoll für ein ländliches Gotteshaus.

The Baroque decoration of the small pilgrimage church in Weissenregen is unusually
fine for a rural place of worship.

^ Kein bayerischer Marktplatz ohne Maibaum:
Hier ein ansehnliches Exemplar im nieder-
bayerischen Deggendorf.

No Bavarian marketplace is complete with-
out its maypole: this impressive example
stands in Deggendorf in Lower Bavaria.

‹ Ein ungewöhnliches Gotteshaus auf drei-eckigem Grundriss: Die Architektur der Kappl, wie die Wallfahrtskirche zur hl. Drei-faltigkeit in Waldsassen genannt wird, nimmt die Drei symbolisch in Grundriss sowie Anzahl der Türme und Zugänge auf.

An unusual church with a triangular ground plan: the architecture of the Kappl, as the pilgrimage church of the Holy Trinity in Waldsassen is known, also symbolises the sacred number in its three towers and entrances.

⌃ Das freistehende Alte Rathaus schmückt den lang gezogenen Markt von Weiden in der Oberpfalz. Gesäumt ist er von gotischen und barocken Fassaden behäbiger Bürger-häuser, viele mit einem überwölbten Durch-gang zum Innenhof.

The free-standing Old Town Hall embelli-shes the long marketplace in Weiden in the Upper Palatinate, which is lined by the Go-thic and Baroque façades of stately bur-ghers' houses, many of them with a vaulted passage to the inner courtyard.

« Kaum jemand würde im von mittelalterlichem Flair geprägten Neumarkt i. d. Oberpfalz moderne Architektur erwarten. Das Museum Lothar Fischer fügt sich perfekt in die historische Umgebung. Es zeigt das bildhauerische Werk des gebürtigen Oberpfälzers Lothar Fischer (1933–2004).

Modern architecture is rather surprising in the medieval atmosphere of Neumarkt i. d. Oberpfalz. The Museum Lothar Fischer fits perfectly into its historic surroundings. It exhibits the work of the sculptor Lothar Fischer (1933–2004), who was born in the Upper Palatinate.

« »Stadtbrille« wird die Bogenbrücke über die Vils genannt, die als Teil der Stadtbefestigung Ambergs 1454 errichtet wurde.

»The town's glasses« is the name for the arched bridge across the Vils, which was built as part of the defences of Amberg in 1454.

‹ Kallmünz im Altmühltal war bereits im 19. Jahrhundert beliebte Sommerfrische für Literaten und Maler; Wassily Kandinsky lernte hier 1903 Gabriele Münter kennen und lieben.

Kallmünz in the Altmühltal was a summer retreat for writers and artists back in the 19th century; here Vassily Kandinsky met and fell in love with Gabriele Münter in 1903.

» Regensburgs hervorragend erhaltene Altstadt mit der Steinernen Brücke über die Donau und dem imposanten, gotischen Dom zählt zum Unesco-Welterbe.

Regensburg's outstandingly preserved old town with the Stone Bridge across the Danube and the impressive Gothic cathedral is a Unesco World Heritage site.

‹ Mittelalterliche Wohn- oder Geschlechtertürme sind charakteristisch für Regensburgs Altstadt. Der Goldene Turm im Hintergrund zählt zu den höchsten; auch das Goliathhaus links war früher ein Patrizierturm.

The medieval residential towers of patrician families are a characteristic feature of the old quarter of Regensburg. The Golden Tower in the background is one of the tallest; the Goliath House on the left was once also a patrician tower.

» Der Regensburger Dom, der 1273 begonnen wurde, gilt als bedeutendes Bauwerk der süddeutschen Gotik.

Regensburg Cathedral, on which construction work started in 1273, is regarded as important example of Gothic architecture in south Germany.

‹ Mit der Walhalla über der Donau unweit von Regensburg ehrte der bayerische König Ludwig I. verdiente Deutsche. Ihre Büsten schmücken den einem griechischen Tempel nachempfundenen Bau.

In Valhalla above the Danube near Regensburg, King Ludwig I of Bavaria honoured eminent Germans. A building based on a Greek temple is adorned with their busts.

In der Weltenburger Enge zwischen Kelheim ›
und dem Kloster Weltenburg durchbrachen
mehrere Nebenflüsse der Donau eine Barrie-
re aus Jurakalk. Später bahnte sich der
Hauptarm seinen Weg durch die so vorberei-
tete Passage, die sich mit bis zu 80 Meter hohen Felswänden auf bis 110 Meter verengt.

In the Weltenburg Gap between Kelheim
and Weltenburg Monastery, several tributa-
ries of the Danube broke through a barrier of
Jurassic limestone. Later the main arm of the
river cut its way through the passage that
had thus been prepared, and is 110 metres
wide at its narrowest point with rock walls
up to 80 metres high.

˄ Nahezu senkrechte Felswände und zu bizarren Formen erodierter Kalkstein wie hier bei Dollnstein bilden im Altmühltal ein anspruchsvolles Kletterrevier aller Schwierigkeitsgrade.

Near Dollnstein the almost vertical rock walls and eroded limestone have created bizarre shapes that make the Altmühltal a challenging climbing terrain for all abilities.

» Hinter den Mauern der Burg Trausnitz oberhalb von Landshut verbirgt sich die kuriose Kunst- und Wunderkammer.

Behind the walls of Trausnitz Castle above Landshut lies a cabinet of curiosities and art.

^ König Ludwig I. stiftete 1838 die Befreiungshalle in Kelheim im Gedenken an den Sieg über Napoleon.

King Ludwig I was the patron of the Hall of Liberation in Kelheim, built in 1838 to commemorate victory over Napoleon.

BILDNACHWEIS | PHOTO CREDITS

TITELBILD | COVER — Bildagentur Huber/Schmid: Seealpsee am Nebelhorn

BUCHRÜCKSEITE | BACK — DuMont Bildarchiv/Campo: Siegestor in München
Bildagentur Huber/Schmid: Bayerische Brotzeit
Bildagentur Huber/Schmid: Donaudurchbruch am Kloster Weltenburg bei Kelheim

INNEN | INSIDE — Bildagentur Huber/Alfeld: 109 o.; Bäck: 3 o., 4/5, 36/37, 41 o.; Cassaro: 78 M., 83 M.; Friedel: 12 o.; Gräfenhain: 19, 24 o., 28, 66 o.re.; Huber: 3 M.o.,16/17, 30, 39 o., 39 u., 48 u.li.; Kornblum: 79; Kreder: 47 o., 51 u.; Mader: 68 u.li.; Römmelt: 3 u., 32 u., 88/89; Schmid: 3 M., 3 M.u., 6, 7 o., 8 o., 8 u., 14, 21, 22/23, 25 u., 27, 31 u., 32 o., 34, 37 u., 43, 44/45, 48 o.re., 48/49, 52 o., 61 o., 61 u., 64/65, 68 u.re., 68/69, 75, 76 u., 77 o., 77 u., 78 o., 78 u., 80, 82, 83 u., 84 o., 84 u., 84/85, 86/87, 91 u., 94 o., 94 u., 96 u., 97, 102 u., 105 o., 106/107; Siebig: 37 o., 94/95, 108/109

DuMont Bildarchiv/Campo: 9, 11 o.; Eisele: 24 u., 29 o., 31 o., 32/33, 35 o., 35 u., 38 o., 38 u., 40, 41 u., 42; Heimbach: 56 u.; Kluyver: 7 u.; Kolley: 62 o.; Kreder: 52 u., 52/53, 54, 55, 56 o., 57 o., 57 u., 58, 59 o., 59 u., 60/61, 62 u., 63; Lueger: 26 u., 46, 109 u.; Maeritz: 73 o.; Scheibner: 66 o.li., 70 o., 70 u., 71, 81 o., 81 u.; Teschner: 76 o.; transit/Hirth: 92 o., 93, 96 o., 98, 104 o., 104 u.; Widmann: 26 M.

glow images/Albert: 11u.; Auth: 12 u.; Bahnmueller: 50 o.; Bail: 50 u., 51 o.; Bottari: 15 u.; Heine: 10/11; Hetz: 7 M.; Irlmeier: 20 o.; Keller: 48 u.re.; Kreutzer: 85; Mayall: 18; Meyer zur Capellen: 66 u.li.; Moxter: 25 o., 48 o.li.; Nachtmann: 67; Siepmann: 26 o., 47 u., 68 o.li.; SuperStock: 13; Szyszka: 66 u.re.

laif/Brunner: 83 o.; Hub: 73 u.; Kirchner: 92 u.; Riehle: 20 u.; Standl: 102 o.; Steinhilber: 90, 100; Volk: 103

look/Zielske: 15 o., 24 M.

mauritius/age: 72; Beck: 29 u.; BY: 105 u.; Hackenberg: 99; Imagebroker: 91 o.; Imagebroker / BAO: 101; Knöll: 68 o.re.; Peters: 74 o.; Siepmann: 74 u.

IMPRESSUM | IMPRINT

COVERGESTALTUNG | COVER LAYOUT
Ingo Juergens, Südgrafik, Stuttgart

BILD- & TEXTREDAKTION, SATZ | EDITOR
Lisa Muntjewerf, Susanne Völler, Anne Winterling, Köln

TEXT | TEXT
Daniela Schetar, München

ÜBERSETZUNG | TRANSLATION
John Sykes, Köln

KARTE | MAP
DuMont Reisekartografie, Fürstenfeldbruck

REPRO | REPRO
Pre Print Partner GmbH & Co. KG, Köln

DRUCK | PRINT
Printed in China

4. Auflage 2022 |
4th edition 2022
ISBN 978-3-7701-8945-8
© DuMont Reiseverlag GmbH & Co. KG,
Marco-Polo-Str. 1, 73760 Ostfildern
www.dumontreise.de

FSC
www.fsc.org
MIX
Papier aus verantwortungsvollen Quellen
FSC® C020056